LORD OF THE FLIES

AN AQA ESSAY WRITING GUIDE

R. P. DAVIS

CONTENTS

FOREWORD

In your GCSE English Literature exam, you will be presented with two questions on William Golding's *Lord of the Flies*, and you will then be asked to pick just one to answer. Of course, once you've picked the question you prefer, there are many methods you might use to tackle it. However, there is one particular technique which, due to its sophistication, most readily allows students to unlock the highest marks: namely, the thematic method.

To be clear, this study guide is not intended to walk you through the novel chapter-by-chapter and sequence-by-sequence: there are many great guides out there that do just that. No, this guide, by sifting through a series of mock exam questions, will demonstrate how to organise a response thematically and thus write a stellar essay: a skill we believe no other study guide adequately covers!

I have encountered students who have structured their essays all sorts of ways: some who'll write about the novel chronologically, others who'll give each character their own paragraph.

The method I'm advocating, on the other hand, involves picking out three to four themes that will allow you to holistically answer the question: these three to four themes will become the three to four content paragraphs of your essay, cushioned between a brief introduction and conclusion. Ideally, these themes will follow from one to the next to create a flowing argument. Within each of these thematic paragraphs, you can then ensure you are jumping through the mark scheme's hoops.

So to break things down further, each thematic paragraph will include various point-scoring components. In each paragraph, you will include quotes from the novel (yes, that means you'll have to have some committed to memory!), offer analyses of these quotes, then discuss how the specific language techniques you have identified illustrate the theme you're discussing. And in most every paragraph, you will comment on the era in which the novel was written and how that helps to understand the chosen theme.

A Goldingesque pig-head sculpture in Assiniboine Park, Winnipeg. Copyright © Rob Swystun.

Don't worry if this all feels daunting. Throughout this guide, I will be illustrating in great detail – by means of examples – how to build an essay of this kind.

The beauty of the thematic approach is that, once you have your themes, you suddenly have a direction and a trajectory, and this makes essay writing a whole lot easier. However, it must also be noted that selecting themes in the first place is something students often find tricky. I have come across many candidates who understand the novel inside out; but when they are presented with questions under exam conditions, and the pressure kicks in, they find it tough to break their response down into themes. The fact of the matter is: the process is a creative one and the best themes require a bit of imagination.

In this guide, I shall take eight different exam-style questions, and shall put together a plan for each – a plan that illustrates in detail how we will be satisfying the mark scheme's criteria. Please do keep in mind that, when operating under timed conditions, your plans will necessarily be less detailed than those that appear in this volume.

Now, you might be asking whether three or four themes is best. The truth is, you should do whatever you feel most comfortable with: the examiner is looking for an original, creative answer, and not sitting there counting the themes. So if you think you are quick enough to cover four, then great. However, if you would rather do three to make sure you do each theme justice, that's also fine. I sometimes suggest that my student pick four themes, but make the fourth one smaller – sort of like an afterthought, or an observation that turns things on their head. That way, if they feel they won't have time to explore this fourth theme in its own right, they can always give it a quick mention in the conclusion instead.

The plaque at Bishop Wordsworth's School in Salisbury –
where Golding taught from 1945 to 1962. Copyright © San
Diego Bill

Before I move forward in earnest, I believe it to be worthwhile
to run through the four Assessment Objectives the exam board
want you to cover in your response – if only to demonstrate
how effective the thematic response can be. I would argue that
the first Assessment Objective (AO1) – the one that wants
candidates to 'read, understand and respond to texts' and
which is worth 12 of the total 30 marks up for grabs – will be
wholly satisfied by selecting strong themes, then fleshing them
out with quotes. Indeed, when it comes to identifying the top
scoring candidates for AO1, the mark scheme explicitly tells
examiners to look for a 'critical, exploratory, conceptualized
response' that makes 'judicious use of precise references' – the
word 'concept' is a synonym of theme, and 'judicious refer-

ences' simply refers to quotes that appropriately support the theme you've chosen.

The second Assessment Objective (AO2) – which is also responsible for 12 marks – asks students to 'analyse the language, form and structure used by a writer to create meanings and effects, using relevant subject terminology where appropriate.' As noted, you will already be quoting from the novel as you back up your themes, and it is a natural progression to then analyse the language techniques used. In fact, this is far more effective than simply observing language techniques (metaphor here, alliteration there), because by discussing how the language techniques relate to and shape the theme, you will also be demonstrating how the writer 'create[s] meanings and effects.'

Now, in my experience, language analysis is the most important element of AO2 – perhaps 8 of the 12 marks will go towards language analysis. You will also notice, however, that AO2 asks students to comment on 'form and structure.' Again, the thematic approach has your back – because though simply jamming in a point on form or structure will feel jarring, when you bring these points up while discussing a theme, as a means to further a thematic argument, you will again organically be discussing the way it 'create[s] meanings and effects.'

AO3 requires you to 'show understanding of the relationships between texts and the contexts in which they were written' and is responsible for a more modest 6 marks in total. These are easy enough to weave into a thematic argument; indeed, the theme gives the student a chance to bring up context in a relevant and fitting way. After all, you don't want it to look like you've just shoehorned a contextual factoid into the mix.

Finally, you have AO4 – known also as "spelling and gram-mar." There are four marks up for grabs here. Truth be told, this guide is not geared towards AO4. My advice? Make sure you are reading plenty of books and articles, because the more you read, the better your spelling and grammar will be. Also, before the exam, perhaps make a list of words you struggle to spell but often find yourself using in essays, and commit them to memory.

Polish cover-art for Golding's *Lord of the Flies*.
Copyright © Louis Wood

My hope is that this book, by demonstrating how to select rele-vant themes, will help you feel more confident in doing so your-self. I believe it is also worth mentioning that the themes I have picked out are by no means definitive. Asked the very same question, someone else may pick out different themes, and write an answer that is just as good (if not better!). Obviously the exam is not likely to be fun – my memory of them is pretty much the exact opposite. But still, this is one of the very few chances that you will get at GCSE level to actually be creative. And to my mind at least, that was always more enjoyable – if enjoyable is the right word – than simply demonstrating that I had memorised loads of facts.

ESSAY PLAN ONE

HOW FAR DOES GOLDING PRESENT RALPH AS A HERO IN LORD OF THE FLIES?

Introduction

I often suggest kicking off the introduction with a piece of historical or literary context, because this ensures you are scoring AO3 marks (marks that too often get neglected!) right off the bat. It's then a good idea to quickly touch on the themes you are planning to discuss, since this will alert the examiner to the fact that AO1 is also front and centre in your mind.

"The concept of individual heroism took a major hit in the wake of WW2: the horrors of the Holocaust had instilled a sense of profound individual powerlessness, while America's bombing of Hiroshima and Nagasaki, framed by many as a kind of paradoxical righteous atrocity, emphasised the moral murkiness of the modern world. Ralph is in many ways a product of this historical moment: while he might be considered heroic insofar as his mission to maintain the social fabric and ensure the boys' rescue might be considered moral, his personal moral code at times seems fungible, while his ability to exert agency is often compromised by group dynamics."[1]

Theme/Paragraph One: Ralph might be deemed heroic insofar as he leads in a way that acknowledges the moral imperative of ensuring the boys' safety and securing their collective rescue.

- Immediately following the assembly in Chapter Two, the boys – rallying around Jack – rush to build a fire that quickly gets out of hand, and in all likelihood kills the boy with the 'mulberry-coloured birthmark.' In contrast, Ralph's attempts to lead after this calamity – with his emphasis on building shelters and maintaining a controlled fire that will boost their chances of rescue ('if we have a signal...they'll come') – represents a kind of moral leadership that prioritises the boys' safety. [*AO1 for advancing the argument with a judiciously selected quote.*]
- While the opprobrium Ralph levels at Jack (after Jack's negligently allows the signal fire to falter while a ship passes by) is in part borne of Ralph's personal desire to escape the island, there is also moral indignation in his fury, and a concern for the greater good: Ralph's language – 'they might have seen us'; 'we might have gone home' – puts the good of the collective ('us'; 'we') at the forefront.[2] Significantly, after Ralph rejects Jack's apology, Golding gives us an insight into the other boys' perception of events: we are told that they believed that 'Jack had done the

decent thing' and that this put 'Ralph, obscurely, in the wrong.' By articulating the children's warped, naïve moral code – a code whose nonsensicality is given away by the idea Ralph is only 'obscurely' in the wrong: wrong in a way that is unclear and uncertain – Golding in fact invites us to ponder the true moral dimensions at play: the fact that Jack has transgressed against the group, and that Ralph holds the morally righteous position.[3] [*AO1 for advancing the argument with a judiciously selected quote; AO2 for the close analysis of the language.*]

- Ralph's focus on maintaining a signal fire that might yield a rescue continues to be a constant refrain: in the penultimate chapter he decries Jack's 'cooking fire' that would fail to alert 'a ship out there'. Thus, insofar as morally righteous conduct might be considered heroic, Ralph's efforts to secure the rescue of the entire party – even as they turn against him – surely casts him as a hero. [*AO1 for advancing the argument with a judiciously selected quote; AO2 for discussing how structure shapes meaning.*]

Theme/Paragraph Two: While Ralph may lead in a way that is morally virtuous, and thus arguably heroic, there are times when this moral heroism is undercut by deeply problematic conduct.

- In perhaps the most poignant moment in the opening chapter, Piggy – in a quiet aside – reprimands the newly elected Ralph for revealing his embarrassing nickname ('I said not to tell') and Ralph gauges that Piggy is 'hurt and crushed'.[4] Yet Ralph is unrepentant: 'Better Piggy than Fatty' he replies, and Golding adds the ironic observation that this cruel shrug-off was said 'with the directness of genuine leadership.'[*AO1 for advancing the argument with a judiciously selected quote; AO2 for the close analysis of the language.*]

- This lapse in morality is, however, the thin end of the wedge, and Ralph on multiple occasions finds himself morally compromised – especially on occasions when swept up by the excesses of the group. His complicity in the mock-hunting of Robert is a case in point: the reader is told that, despite the fact Robert was 'screaming and struggling' in genuine fear, Ralph fought 'to get near, to get a handful of that brown vulnerable flesh' – that loaded word 'flesh' indicating how Ralph, in tandem with the other hunters, had dehumanised Robert, and reduced him to meat. This incident of course prefigures the murder of Simon in 'A View to a Death', in which Ralph is again complicit; again swept up by the immoral frenzy of the group.[5] Golding notes how 'Piggy and Ralph...found themselves eager to take a place in this demented' gathering, and thus became part of the 'single organism' that takes Simon's life. [*AO1 for advancing the argument with a judiciously selected quote; AO2 for the close analysis of the language.*]

- Yet while Ralph's complicity in these increasingly depraved events may compromise our perception of him as hero, it ought to be noted that classical notions of heroism often demand that a hero be flawed: Aristotle argued that a tragic hero ought to have a *hamartia*: a tragic character flaw. If Ralph's deep-seated need to be accepted by the group might be considered his *hamartia*, it might in turn be argued that it in fact enhances his status as hero. [*AO3 for placing the text in literary context.*]

Theme/Paragraph Three: As Jack secedes from Ralph's party and increasingly becomes the novel's villain, Ralph's opposition to Jack increasingly casts him as the hero.

- In the latter half of the novel, after Ralph, Jack and Roger encounter the airman on the mountaintop and mistake him for a beast, Jack secedes from Ralph's miniature society, and leads his own cohort with dictatorial menace: the reader learns, for instance, how torture is incorporated into Jack's method of governance ('He's going to beat Wilfred'), and how even Jack's loyalists recognise this as 'irresponsible authority'.[6] [*AO1 for advancing the argument with a judiciously selected quote.*]
- Golding has explicitly noted that he intended Jack's breakaway cohort to be interpreted as a reincarnation of the Nazi movement: he observes how he 'took English boys and said, "Look, this could be you."' As a result, Ralph and his society of the conch – a symbol of constitutionalism as opposed to tyranny – becomes the *de facto* allied forces, locked in a heroic Manichean struggle with his fascist counterparts.[7] [*AO3 for placing the text in historical context.*]
- Yet while Golding may have wished to cast Jack's society as Naziesque, he in fact describes them in terms that are reminiscent of colonial caricatures of black natives: Jack becomes the 'chief', and his acolytes 'savages' and 'painted n*****s'. Indeed, when Jack applies 'charcoal' to his face, it appears that he is

not merely adopting blackface; he is "going native", morphing into the regressive black man of the colonial imagination. Golding is thus also casting Ralph and Piggy as the white colonialists, attempting to subdue Jack's "native" pseudo-society.[8] While a 1950s audience might have still construed this endeavour as heroic, a post-colonial reading understands that the depiction of black natives is false in the first place – a mechanism to excuse subjugation – and thus that Ralph's heroism here is predicated on a false premise. [*AO1 for advancing the argument with a judiciously selected quote; AO2 for the close analysis of the language; AO3 for placing the text in historical context.*]

Theme/Paragraph Four: Ralph is presented as the hero insofar as the narrative revolves around him, and the narrator hews closely to his point of view.

- Golding starts his novel with his lens clearly focused on Ralph: the opening sentence talks of 'the boy with fair hair' who 'began to pick his way towards the lagoon.' As the novel unfolds, Golding continues in this vein, for though he uses the third person, his free indirect style ensures that for the lion's share of the novel we are inside Ralph's head, with a front-row seat to his stuttering thoughts – the oft-repeated 'because, because', for instance, neatly capturing his attempts to grapple with complexity.[9] [*AO1 for advancing the argument with a judiciously selected quote; AO2 for the close analysis of the language and for discussing how form shapes meaning.*]
- The narrative technique implicitly invites the reader

to empathise with Ralph, to vicariously decipher the world from his viewpoint, thereby casting him as the hero in the reader's imagination: the one for whom the reader roots above all others.

Conclusion

We have a meaty essay here; so, instead of introducing new ideas, I have decided to invoke another text from the 1950s as I wrap things up, thereby ensuring I pick up any spare AO3 (historical context) marks that might be going spare.

"In John Wyndham's *Plan for Chaos* (another early 1950s novel), the protagonist surreally finds himself doing battle with neo-Nazi clones of himself – a paradoxical setup that somehow casts him both as hero and villain; both the central, all-important figure, but also just a powerless one-of-many. While perhaps not to the same degree, Ralph's position is also deeply equivocal: he is the protagonist and the heroic moral beacon, yet also morally compromised, powerless in the face of the group.[10] At one point, one of the littluns says he 'started to call out for Ralph' when scared at night: like the littlun, the reader imagines Ralph as the hero, yet in various ways he is presented as falling short of the heroic ideal."

A promotional image for the Shetland Youth Theatre's 2012 production of *Lord of the Flies.* Copyright © Shetland Arts

ESSAY PLAN TWO

HOW FAR DOES GOLDING PRESENT SIMON AS AN OUTSIDER IN LORD OF THE FLIES?

Introduction

Again, you'll notice that I'm kicking the essay off with a bid for those AO3 marks – this time, by trying to place the text in its literary context and discussing the prevalence of outsiders in twentieth century literature/film. I then pivot to the themes in *Lord of the Flies* I'm intending to cover, thus alerting the examiner to the AO1 ideas I have in mind.

"The outsider is a recurrent trope in twentieth century cultural products – be it the isolated narrator of T. S. Eliot's 'J. Alfred Prufrock', the exiled Kinbote in Nabokov's *Pale Fire* (1962), or the Tramp of Charlie Chaplin's enormously popular films. Simon in Golding's *Lord of the Flies* encompasses many hallmarks of the outsider: not only in that he seems to physically exist on the peripheries – the staging telegraphing his outsider status – but also in the ways in which he seems incomprehensible to others. Yet insofar as Simon comes to represent certain "beastly" qualities that lie within *all* the boys, he is also paradoxically at the heart (*not* the peripheries) of the book's affairs."

Theme/Paragraph One: The novel's staging often seems to cast Simon as an outsider and a loner: he is time and again found physically stalking the peripheries.

- When the reader first encounters Simon, he arrives as a member of the 'choir' arriving 'in step in two parallel lines', yet soon finds himself falling foul of this organised formation: he faints and 'flopped on his face in the sand and the line broke up.' The alliteration of 'flopped' and face' coupled with the explicit acknowledgement that 'the line broke up' draws attention to this early micro-instance of Simon becoming physically removed from the rest of the cohort. [*AO1 for advancing the argument with a judiciously selected quote; AO2 for the close analysis of the language.*]

- Indeed, as the novel progresses, Simon is increasingly found on the physical peripheries. Crucially, he develops a habit of extricating himself from the camp – the boys' centre of civilisation – and absconding to his secret clearing 'where the butterflies danced'; and even though 'utterly alone', he physically places himself at the peripheries of this peripheral clearing: he hides in the 'great mat that hung at the side.' Moreover, not only does he have a habit of heading to this spot at night (and thus leaving the camp at a time when nobody else tends to gallivant), but he also ventures solo through the island's most remote terrain: he opts to walk 'through the forest by himself' in Chapter Seven, and later climbs alone up to the mountain-stranded corpse. After Simon is killed, it is striking how the tide washes his body 'out towards the open sea': the loner-cum-outsider is physically swept 'out' beyond the island's limits. [*AO1 for advancing the argument with a judiciously selected quote; AO2 for the close analysis of the language.*]

Theme/Paragraph Two: By treating Simon as synonymous with the beast while orchestrating his murder, the boys collectively act to cast Simon as the arch-outsider.

- In one of the book's most climactic sequences, the boys – while at a twilight celebration lionising Jack's second successful hunting venture – engage in a mock hunt, which then escalates into something far more real as Simon stumbles onto the scene.[1] From the instant Simon arrives, the frenzied boys urgently begin to cast him as the very 'beast' that had represented an existential threat in their imaginations: in the space of a few lines we are told that 'the beast stumbled'; 'the beast was on his knees'; and 'the beast struggled.'[2] Indeed, that Simon is forced onto 'his knees' symbolically mirrors the way he is being cast as a stooping, non-human "other" – and, even once dispatched, they refuse to acknowledge his humanity: 'the beast lay still.' [*AO1 for advancing the argument with a judiciously selected quote; AO2 for the close analysis of the language.*]

- However, while the boys may in this sequence have sought to cast Simon as the arch-outsider – the beast incarnate – Golding's novel simultaneously emphasises the fallaciousness of this effort.[3] The novel seems to make clear that the elusive beast is in fact a ubiquitous phenomenon: not only are fires, snakes, the dead pilot, and the boars all identified as the 'beast' at one point or another, but Simon himself acknowledges that the 'beast' is in fact a quality that exists within all of them: 'a picture of a human', as Simon sees it.[4] Therefore, if we are to accept the boy's interpretation of Simon as the beast, he is *not* then an outsider, but a symbol of a quality at their collective core.

Theme/Paragraph Three: The secret symmetry between Simon and Ralph – the leader of the boys for much of the novel – problematises any easy categorisation of Simon as an outsider.

- At the end of Chapter Eight, Simon, while domiciled in his enclosed 'mat', has a hallucinatory rendezvous with the pig's head ('the obscene thing') impaled on a stick – the eponymous 'Lord of the Flies'. Four chapters later, however, there is an eerie reprise of the scene, as Ralph also stumbles upon the pig's head, and the skull 'regarded him like one who knows all the answers but won't tell.' Shortly after, when Ralph finds himself fleeing from the others boys, he winds up domiciled in a thick mat made of a 'wild tangle of creeper' – a space deeply reminiscent of the one

Simon sought refuge in. At this point of the novel, Ralph is isolated and on the run, and thus, in a way, by walking in Simon's footsteps, Ralph is not only drawing attention to his newfound outsider status, but also acting to reaffirm Simon as the original outsider. [*AO1 for advancing the argument with a judiciously selected quote; AO2 for the close analysis of the language and for discussing how structure shapes meaning.*]

- Yet as Simon also at times walks in Ralph's footsteps – for instance, where Ralph approaches the dead airman at the end of Chapter Seven, Simon does the same in Chapter Nine – the reader is also invited to grapple with the extent to which Ralph's status for much of the novel as arch-insider and leader might also, in an equal and opposite fashion, be considered to have rubbed off on Simon, thereby thwarting our attempts to categorise Simon as an unequivocal outsider. [*AO2 for discussing how structure shapes meaning.*]

Theme/Paragraph Four: The third-person narrator gives more insight into Simon's internal monologue than most other characters, complicating our perception of him as an outsider.

- In Chapter Four, the reader learns of Jack's first successful kill; however, although one would imagine that the kill itself might have made for an exciting sequence, the narrator chooses *not* to recount it – rather, the reader learns of the kill after the event, as Jack brings Ralph up to speed: 'We've killed a pig.' [*AO2 for discussing how form shapes meaning.*]

- This choice alerts the reader to the ways in which the third-person narrator, by rarely elaborating on Jack's subjective viewpoint, in fact casts Jack as an outsider to the reader. By contrast, the third person narrator's free indirect technique *does* on a number of occasions delve into Simon's subjective experience. For instance, the reader is given an insight into Simon's meditations on the beast: 'However Simon thought of the beast, there arose before his inward sight the picture of a human.' The phrase 'inward sight' is particularly significant, for the reader is getting a front-row seat to the 'inward' realm of Simon's mind. Yet this is just one of a number of instances this happens: we learn of Simon's insecurities; we follow him to his clearing; we follow him up the mountain. [*AO1 for advancing the argument with a judiciously selected quote; AO2 for the close analysis of the language.*]
- Yet while the third person narrator complicates Simon's outsider status by providing a window into his interior world, one might observe how Simon also struggles to make this interior world know to the other boys: he contemplates his inability to 'stand and speak' due to the 'dreadful... pressure of personality.' While the narrator familiarises the reader to Simon, Simon is unable to make himself familiar to the boys. [*AO1 for advancing the argument with a judiciously selected quote.*]

Conclusion

You can score contextual (AO3) marks by invoking texts that may not be from the same era, but which we know to have influenced the writer. Here, I invoke Shakespeare's *The Tempest*, which influenced Golding's writing of *Lord of the Flies* in a number of ways.

"In Shakespeare *The Tempest* (a text with which Golding was deeply familiar) Caliban is repeatedly labelled a monster by other characters, while these characters ironically themselves engage in monstrous behaviour. In a sense, Simon is involved in a similar dynamic: he is cast by the boys as arch-outsider – a beast – yet it is his peers' murderous conduct towards him that is truly monstrous. In fact, whereas Caliban is tarred by an attempted rape, Simon has no such mark by his name, and is seemingly far less vicious than his peers. Thus if this so-called beast ought to be a considered an outsider, it is perhaps foremost as a *moral* outlier: Simon is least bestial of them all."

Johann Heinrich Ramberg's depiction of Shakespeare's so-called monstrous Caliban (far left) dancing with two other characters: Stephano and Tinculo.

ESSAY PLAN THREE

WHAT IS THE SIGNIFICANCE OF HUNTING IN LORD OF THE FLIES?

INTRODUCTION

Once again, I'm kicking off the essay by placing the text in literary context (and scoring AO3 marks in the process) – though whereas in the previous introduction I touched on a number of other texts, on this occasion I hone in on just one and use it as a springboard.

"In John Wyndham's *Web*, a novel from the late 1950s, a group of British explorers find themselves stranded on a remote Pacific island and systematically hunted by a kind of beast: a pack of predatory spiders. While anxieties about being hunted by some theoretical island 'beast' also pervade Golding's *Lord of the Flies*, it is the children, galvanised by Jack, who in fact become the island's hunters, and this pursuit figures powerfully as a way for the boys to enact an idealised version of manhood. Yet as the novel progresses and the animal bloodletting becomes more routine, the hunting starts to create a permissive atmosphere that leads to escalating violence."

Theme/Paragraph One: The hunting is significant to the boys because it figures as a way to prove their strength, cunning and power – and their capacity to enact an idealised version of manhood.

- Just after Ralph wins election in Chapter One, there is a suggestion that Jack's choir could be either 'the army' or 'hunters;' and by Chapter Two the two classifications have become interchangeable: as Jack puts it, 'you need an army – for hunting.' This conflation gives insight to how the boys construe hunting. During WW2, army service became synonymous with courage, virtue, and manliness in popular discourse, and thus, by linking hunting and the army, the boys act to elevate it to a kind of rite of passage, an arch symbol of manliness. [*AO1 for advancing the argument with a judiciously selected quote; AO2 for the close analysis of the language; AO3 for placing the text in historical context.*]

- Although Jack figures as the novel's most prominent hunter, his mentality – that one might demonstrate their machismo and leadership bona-fides through hunting – proves pervasive.[1] Indeed, even Ralph (who had vocally derided hunting earlier in the novel) finds himself swelling with pride in Chapter Seven after injuring a boar with a spear. Crucially, not only does Golding's narrator observe that Ralph 'felt the need of witnesses' – thereby revealing Ralph's innate sense of the value of hunting as a spectacle, as a means of demonstrating manliness to external 'witnesses' – but the narrator also remarks on the other boys' 'new respect' for Ralph, indicating that they do indeed deem this spectacle to be proof of some inner manliness. [*AO1 for advancing the argument with a judiciously selected quote; AO2 for the close analysis of the language.*]

- Later in the novel still, Jack berates the 'littluns' as 'cry-babies and sissies' because they 'don't hunt or build.' In this formulation, those who do not hunt are to be considered infantile ('cry-babies) and effeminate ('sissies') – an all-but-explicit indication of how hunting figures in the novel as a means for the older boys to enact an idealised version of manhood predicated on strength, bravery and violence. [*AO1 for advancing the argument with a judiciously selected quote; AO2 for the close analysis of the language.*]

Theme/Paragraph Two: Hunting stands in opposition to fire as symbols of the power struggle between Jack and Ralph: whereas hunting is Jack's priority, maintaining a signal fire is Ralph's.

- That the power struggle between Ralph and Jack will be a significant component of the novel is hinted at by Golding's structural choice to have them vie for election in the opening chapter; and their divergent priorities – that is, Ralph's desire to maintain a signal fire ('we must make a fire'), and Jack's desire to hunt – are established almost immediately, thus setting them up as symbols of the power struggle. Indeed, in Chapter Four, Golding ensures that these priorities do

not just diverge, but actively clash, as Jack and his
hunters – who had taken responsibility for the fire
('we'll be responsible for keeping the fire going') –
allow the fire to falter while on a hunt, causing the
boys to miss an opportunity to alert a passing ship.
[*AO1 for advancing the argument with a judiciously
selected quote; AO2 for the close analysis of the
language and for discussing how structure shapes
meaning.*]

- In the showdown that follows, Golding seems to make
explicit the status of hunting and fire as symbols for
Jack and Ralph respectively: after observing that 'the
two boys faced each other,' the narrator, in the very
next sentence, observes that 'there was the brilliant
world of hunting...; and there was the world of...
commonsense,' as if the 'hunting' were
interchangeable with Jack, and 'commonsense' –
which the narrator here links to the fire – with Ralph.
Indeed, the semi-colon halfway through this sentence,
breaking it in two, ensures that the sentence's form
reflects the dichotomy between Ralph and Jack;
between fire and hunting. That hunting and fire
become a stand-in for the two boys' opposing
mentality is picked up by the other characters, too: as
Piggy observes, 'If Jack was chief he'd have all hunting
and no fire.' [*AO1 for advancing the argument with a
judiciously selected quote; AO2 for the close analysis
of the language.*]

- Interestingly, in the novel denouement, not only does
Jack wield the hunt against Ralph as a way to
reconcile his power – to eliminate Ralph altogether –
but he also appropriates fire and uses it against
Ralph.[2] Yet, ironically, the ensuing forest fire leads to

the boys' rescue, and offers a final vindication for Ralph: the fire – *not* the hunt – ends up being their path to salvation after all.

Theme/Paragraph Three: The hunting of animals normalises violence among the boys, and acts as a kind of gateway to escalating violence between the boys.

- In Chapter Two, although the threat of violence is introduced when Jack, Ralph and Simon come across a pig tangled in a thicket and Jack draws his knife, Jack does not act because – as the narrator puts it – 'of the enormity of the knife cutting into living flesh'. While this sequence is unnerving – especially as it seems to foreshadow violence against the very much human Piggy the reader has met the chapter beforehand – the boys are still governed by forces that render outright violence a taboo: the residual influence 'of parents and school and policemen and the law.'[3] [*AO1 for advancing the argument with a judiciously selected quote.*]
- However, after Jack's first successful kill, there appears to be a normalisation of violence that spills over into how the boys treat one another: the mock-hunt of Robert, which spirals into Robert 'squeal[ing]' in 'real pain', is a case in point. Indeed, this pattern repeats itself (though in escalating fashion) in the wake of Jack's second successful hunt in Chapter Eight, which primes the children to engage in the murder of Simon in the very next chapter; and the way Simon is characterised as an animal – 'the thing was crawling'; 'the beast stumbled' – strengthens the

notion that the hunting of the animals directly leads to the hunting of one another. [*AO1 for advancing the argument with a judiciously selected quote; AO2 for the close analysis of the language and for discussing how structure shapes meaning.*]

- The evolution of the word 'flesh' throughout the novel is particularly instructive when assessing this link. At first, the word is reserved for animals, such as the pig's 'living flesh' in Chapter Two. Yet the word crops up during the mock-hunt of Robert, with reference to his 'brown, vulnerable flesh' – as if, in the wake of the first kill, the boys are increasingly seeing one another as lumps of meat – and, by the time Ralph is being hunted during the novel's climax, there are multiple references to his flesh: 'flesh over Ralph's ribs'; 'bruised flesh'. [*AO1 for advancing the argument with a judiciously selected quote; AO2 for the close analysis of the language and for discussing how structure shapes meaning.*]

Conclusion

Although my essay here covers a number of themes, I have one more I'd like to cover – namely, the children's paranoia about being hunted – so I've worked it into my conclusion.

"At one point, Jack – while describing his hunting expedition – observes that he at times felt 'as if [he's] not hunting, but – being hunted.' This draws attention to another way hunting figures in Golding's novel – namely, the way the boys experience anxiety about *being* hunted by some fictional, external entity – and this, as opposed to their own hunting efforts, is significant in a different way: in reminding us of the collective youth of these islanders who believe in fantastic beasts. Yet while this paranoia may point to their youth, it might also be seen to chime with the far more justified paranoia felt by many in the immediate wake of the excesses of the Nazi regime."

Another iteration of cover art for *Lord of the Flies*. Copyright © Wolf Gang

ESSAY PLAN FOUR

HOW DOES GOLDING PRESENT PIGGY AS A SIGNIFICANT CHARACTER IN LORD OF THE FLIES?

Introduction

"In the wake of WW2, there was a proliferation of fictions that sought to place the naivety of childhood in distressing situations: for instance, John Barth's 1968 short story, 'Lost in the Funhouse', combines its protagonist's coming-of-age trauma with an episode of entrapment in an amusement park's funhouse. Of all the children subject to the considerably more distressing entrapment on Golding's island in *Lord of the Flies*, however, Piggy is arguably presented as least naïve, and becomes particularly significant as the mouthpiece for principles of democratic rule and rationality. Yet when Piggy is occasionally seen to lapse into childhood naivety, these moments become significant, too: as potent reminders of the gulf between childhood and adulthood."

Theme/Paragraph One: Piggy is significant as the chief advocate for the principles of democratic rule and rational decision making – concepts which come to be embodied by the conch he so prizes.

- When Piggy first sets eyes on the conch in Chapter One, it galvanises his instincts to organise and establish rational rule: he asserts that 'we can use this to call the others' and 'have a meeting.' Shortly after, the conch becomes linked not only with the decision to hold a vote (the narrator observes that 'the toy of voting was almost as pleasing as the conch', implicitly creating an equivalence between the two), but also decorous decision making: it becomes the mechanism for indicating who has the floor. [*AO1 for advancing the argument with a judiciously selected quote; AO2 for the close analysis of the language.*]

- If Piggy and the conch he prizes become significant as symbols of democratic rule, this significance is only enhanced when Jack later forms a group centred on dictatorial 'irresponsible leadership' that explicitly defines itself in opposition to the conch: Jack states pointedly his ambition to 'get more of the biguns away from the conch'. Given that Golding intended Jack's breakaway cohort to be a kind of reincarnation of the Nazi movement, Piggy and his conch are arguably significant as the face not only of democratic principles, but of these principles standing as a bulwark against fascism.[1] [*AO1 for advancing the argument with a judiciously selected quote; AO2 for the close analysis of the language; AO3 for placing the text in historical context.*]

- However, while Golding wished Jack and his breakaway group to be read as Nazis, he in fact portrays them in ways reminiscent of colonial caricatures of black natives: Jack becomes the 'chief'; his 'savage' followers proudly brandish spears; and his acolytes (in Piggy's own words) become 'painted n*****s'. Golding was writing at a time of defensive justification of Britain's empire, with mainstream voices aggressively seeking to double down on the notion that it had been a virtuous effort to civilise "uncivilised" peoples. In light of this, Piggy and his conch could arguably be perceived less as democratic symbols, and more as symbols of Golding's rosy view of colonialism, which – through his caricature portrayal of native peoples – he seems to cast as a necessary "civilising" force. [*AO1 for advancing the argument with a judiciously selected quote; AO2 for the close analysis of the language; AO3 for placing the text in historical context.*]

Theme/Paragraph Two: Although Piggy is frequently portrayed (and even strives to define himself) as the most "adult" of the children, he is also significant in drawing attention to the gulf between childhood and adulthood.

- In Chapter One, the reader is given a strikingly in-depth portrait of Piggy: we learn of his 'asthma' which gives him a distinct air of infirmity (he was 'breathing hard'); his fastidious manner ('he wiped his glasses');

and his world-weary expression ('expression of pain and concentration'). While a child, Golding seems to present Piggy *physically* as though having some of the markers one might associate with adulthood. [*AO1 for advancing the argument with a judiciously selected quote; AO2 for the close analysis of the language.*]

- On top of this, though, Piggy also seems to *define himself* as adult. In Chapter Two, immediately after Jack overrides the proceedings to recklessly start a fire, Piggy remarks 'scornfully' that they are behaving 'like kids' – by contrast implicitly casting himself as "adult". Significantly, however, what Piggy seems to be deriding as childish appears not just to be a rash way of conducting affairs, but a kind of fantasist mentality – a deluded conviction that they have been dropped into some kind of fiction – that seems to touch all the boys but Piggy. Indeed, just prior to the fire sequence – in a moment that arguably creates the permissive atmosphere that allows it to happen – Ralph proclaims their situation is 'just like in a book,' to which the others boisterously agree by positing texts: 'Treasure Island'; 'Swallows and Amazons'. Piggy, then, is adult insofar as he is keen instead to occupy reality. This is perhaps best exemplified by his lack of credulity towards the 'beast'. Whereas the other boys believe in things that go bump in the night (and even Ralph is credulous: 'are there ghosts, Piggy? Or beasts?'), Piggy remains philosophically wedded to reality: 'course there aren't'. [*AO1 for advancing the argument with a judiciously selected quote; AO2 for the close analysis of the language.*]

- Yet while *philosophically* rational, at times of extreme stress even Piggy occasionally checks his commitment to reality at the door: during Jack's night-time glasses heist, for instance, the bewildered Piggy is momentarily credulous: 'It's come!...It's real!' Moreover, when explaining to Ralph how he knows beasts and ghosts to be fictional, Piggy struggles to articulate himself: Piggy offers a non-sequitur – the beast cannot exist because 'Houses an' streets, an' – TV – they wouldn't work' – while his linguistic tics (the refrain on 'an'', the pauses indicated by the dashes either side of 'TV') are stark reminders of Piggy's youth.[2] Thus, while Piggy may stand apart from his peers, his lapses into fantastical thinking and struggles to articulate himself are ultimately reminders of the gulf between childhood and adulthood. [*AO1 for advancing the argument with a judiciously selected quote; AO2 for the close analysis of the language.*]

Theme/Paragraph Three: Piggy is significant insofar as he is crucial in allowing us to decipher the novel's protagonist, Ralph, and decode his moral and symbolic status.

- The novel's opening pages place the lens exclusively on Ralph ('the boy with fair hair') and Piggy ('the fat boy'), a structural choice that telegraphs that Piggy will be crucial to our understanding Ralph – the individual who, through the third person free indirect style, is marked out early as the novel's protagonist. [*AO1 for advancing the argument with a judiciously selected quote; AO2 for discussing how structure shapes meaning.*]
- Whereas Ralph is quickly elected leader in the chapters that follow, and made the centre of the

group, in many respects Piggy becomes the ultimate outsider: he is the only boy deprived of a name ('Piggy' is a derisive nickname); his verbal patter (as exemplified by the double negative of 'nobody don't know we're here') betrays his relative lack of privilege; and his lack of fitness marks him as an outlier. That Ralph chooses to occasionally deride Piggy to gain social capital – be it through the early disclosure of Piggy's nickname, or his willingness to laugh along with Jack's secessionist clan at Piggy's lack of physical dexterity ('Ralph and the boys were united... by a storm of laughter') – is used by Golding to demonstrate a key flaw in Ralph's character: his need for acceptance. Yet that he does in fact side with Piggy indicates to the reader that Ralph is ultimately allied to what Piggy and his conch represent – whether that be democratic norms, colonial myths, or a contradictory mix of the two. [*AO1 for advancing the argument with a judiciously selected quote; AO2 for the close analysis of the language.*]

Conclusion

Again, literary context (AO3) does not always require you to invoke texts from the same era. Shakespeare's *King Lear* is from the early seventeenth century, but since Golding very obviously draws on it, we are safe to use it as a means of picking up context marks.

In Shakespeare's *King Lear*, the freshly blinded Gloucester achieves a new metaphorical clarity regarding the son he betrayed, and resolves to hurl himself off a cliff (an effort thwarted by that very son posing as a vagrant). Piggy figures as a complex rewriting of Gloucester. While blind from the outset – which Golding uses to spell-out Piggy's metaphorical clarity – Piggy is re-blinded for emphasis by Jack's assault on his glasses. Moreover, whereas Gloucester is spared death by his son leading him to a purely fictional cliff-edge, Piggy (in a bleaker rewriting) is forced off a cliff that is all too real. Thus Golding, through this tragic allusion, clearly indicates his desire for Piggy to be read above all as the novel's tragic fulcrum; though *what* has been tragically lost in his death – rationality? empire? democratic norms? – might be debated.[3]

A photoartist's depiction of Piggy. Copyright © Stephen Brace

ESSAY PLAN FIVE

HOW DOES GOLDING PRESENT THE ISLAND AS A CENTRAL CHARACTER IN LORD OF THE FLIES?

INTRODUCTION

Historical context comes in all shapes and sizes. This time, I'm invoking historical context that's relevant to the location in which Golding chose to set his novel, since it links nicely to the essay question we're dealing with.

"Given how the Pacific Ocean through the early twentieth century increasingly came to be seen as a domain to be conquered and experimented with by the world's major powers – this possibly best exemplified by America dropping a hydrogen bomb there in May 1951 – it is perhaps unsurprising that Golding decided to make a remote Pacific island host of his social experiment. Yet while the island features as the novel's indispensable ingredient – the entity which gives the plot its entire impetus – it is also essential to register that there are in fact two islands in the novel: the physical island on which the children are stranded, and the island in their imaginations."

Theme/Paragraph One: Insofar as the island gives the narrative its entire impetus, it might be considered the novel's central, all-important character.

- Crucially, the novel starts at the point at which the children are stranded on the island, and wraps up on the arrival of the ship and its 'the huge peaked cap' – the means by which the children might depart the island. This of course points to the fact that the island is not just significant in the novel, but the crucial means by which it might fulfil its *raison d'être*: namely, to see how a group of British children would fare when cut-off from the adult world and 'the protection of parents and school and policemen and the law.'[1] Indeed, the children seem to understand that whether or not they are on an island is crucial to the narrative arc they will face: 'If this isn't an island we might be rescued straight away,' Ralph observes in the opening chapter, and then states the need – before anything else – to establish this fact definitively. [*AO1 for advancing the argument with a judiciously selected quote; AO2 for the close analysis of the language.*]
- Deploying an island as the central narrative impetus – as a means to confine individuals to a delimited space – is a time-honoured tactic, and Golding alludes to popular iterations, from Shakespeare's *The Tempest* to Ballantyne's *Coral Island*. However, it was particularly in vogue in the decade or so after WW2:

for example, John Wyndham's *Web* (written shortly after *Lord of the Flies*) similarly revolves around Brits stranded on a Pacific island, and similarly takes narrative momentum from their entrapment. Thus, insofar as the source of narrative impetus ought to be considered a text's central character, the island in *Lord of the Flies* is certainty presented as such. [*AO3 for placing the text in historical and literary context.*]

Theme/Paragraph Two: While the physical island on which the children are stranded is presented as a central character in the book, a second island – the one that exists in the children's imagination – is also central in its own right.

- When Ralph holds court in Chapter Two, there is a key moment in which Ralph asserts that their situation is 'just like in a book,' and the other boys agree by citing other texts that feature stranded youths: 'Treasure Island'; 'Swallows and Amazons'. This hints at a dynamic that is crucial to decoding the novel: namely, that while the island is real, the children simultaneously occupy a romanticised fictional island – a realm informed by the islands they have encountered in books – which they superimpose on the real island. [*AO1 for advancing the argument with a judiciously selected quote; AO2 for the close analysis of the language.*]
- Significantly, that the children inhabit this second romanticised island gives them latitude to create fictional roles for themselves. As a result, when Ralph, Jack and Simon explore the island in Chapter One,

they are not just children navigating a physical island, but adventurers interacting with a romanticised version of the island: the repetition of 'Wacco', 'Wizard', 'Smashing' – instances of boyish slang – telegraph not only excitement, but also the fact they are at play in their imaginations. Indeed, part of the children's play is a kind of probing to see how the fictional version of the island in their heads tallies with the physical island before them – hence their fascination in toppling 'the rock...as large as a small motor car' off a cliff. That the imaginary island and the real one of 'pink rocks' are *not* in fact separable, however, leads to problems as the novel unfolds, for roles inspired by the island in the boys' heads (such as that of hunter) take on lives of their own when let loose on the real-world. [*AO1 for advancing the argument with a judiciously selected quote; AO2 for the close analysis of the language.*]

- The island in the boys' imagination is important, too, insofar as it gives space for the fictional 'beast' to thrive. On the real island – if we exclude the boys and the pigs – there are no beasts; there is only a dead airman. Yet the island of the boys' imagination, in which boys can be hunters and explorers and chiefs, also leaves room for beasts. At one point, one boy suggests that 'perhaps... the beast is – a ghost.' In a sense, this is correct: it is a 'ghost' that hails from their imaginary island, and haunts them in the real one. [*AO1 for advancing the argument with a judiciously selected quote; AO2 for the close analysis of the language.*]

Theme/Paragraph Three: The island features as a central character in Golding's warped parable on the virtues of colonialism.

- Once Ralph, Simon and Jack climb the island's mountain for the first time, the narrator observes how, as they surveyed the view, 'they savoured the right of domination.' Seemingly written without irony, this loaded aside casts the boys as young colonialists – the double meaning of 'right' suggesting these young Europeans are not only altogether entitled to control the island, but are also acting with moral righteousness in doing so. Yet if Golding here seems to present the logic of empire as natural and even moral, it is important to note that this attitude very much tallied with mainstream British views of the 1950s: a time when establishment voices were doubling down in their effort to portray colonialism as a virtuous project to civilise "uncivilised" spaces. [*AO1 for advancing the argument with a judiciously selected quote; AO2 for the close analysis of the language; AO3 for placing the text in historical context.*]
- As the novel progresses, however, the island's role in Golding's colonial parable becomes more complex still. Eventually, a group (led by Jack) secede from Ralph's society of the conch; and although Golding has stated that Jack's secessionist society was supposed to be a reincarnation of the Nazi movement, they are portrayed in a way far more reminiscent of colonial caricatures of native people: Jack becomes the 'chief', and his acolytes 'savages' and 'painted n*****s'. As a result, the island for the remaining colonialist becomes not just a landmass to physically colonise,

but a cultural realm that requires philosophical colonising, too. [*AO1 for advancing the argument with a judiciously selected quote; AO2 for the close analysis of the language; AO3 for placing the text in historical context.*]

- When Ralph et al. plan their showdown at castle rock in Chapter Eleven, and they suggest they ought to 'bathe' and 'comb their hair' and put on 'socks', and *not* be 'painted' like 'savages', the symbolism is plain: Golding presents them as heroically pitting the symbols of European civilisation against what colonialists stereotyped as the symbols of native culture. Therefore, if we decide the novel is an effort to justify and aggrandise colonialism, the remote island populated with caricature savages is not just significant, but the all-important character in the narrative. [*AO1 for advancing the argument with a judiciously selected quote; AO2 for the close analysis of the language; AO3 for placing the text in historical context.*]

Conclusion

Another way of tackling the conclusion is to take a quote and go to town with the close language analysis. This is a good way to ensure that you are maxing out on the AO2 front.

"At one point in Chapter Four, Jack appropriates Piggy's glasses to light a fire, and Piggy is left 'islanded in a sea of meaningless colour.' With a single verbal flourish transforming noun to verb, Golding layers all sorts of meanings on the word 'islanded'. Suddenly, to be 'islanded' is to be blinded, and thus the island becomes synonymous not only with failures of sight (a central trope in the novel) but with Piggy himself: in that moment, Piggy and the island become interchangeable, the social isolation of one mirroring that of the other. If this illustrates anything, it is that Golding's success at placing the island at the centre of the text ultimately stems from his ability to invest it with a multitude of meanings, guaranteeing its centrality in any reading of the work."

The aftermath of America's hydrogen bomb
test in the Pacific Ocean in May 1951.

ESSAY PLAN SIX

HOW DOES GOLDING PRESENT HUMAN NATURE IN LORD OF THE FLIES?

INTRODUCTION

"By the mid twentieth century, the ways mankind conceived of itself had been irrevocably altered by the paradigm-shifting writings of such thinkers as Sigmund Freud and Charles Darwin, as well as the tumult of two world wars. The impact of all of these influences – and more – can be felt in Golding's *Lord of the Flies*, a novel deeply interested in how group dynamics shape individual behaviour, but also how exposure to violence desensitises and begets more violence. Yet the novel's meditations on humanity are more varied still, ranging from the power fiction has over the imagination to man's tendency to define oneself and others by appearances."

Theme/Paragraph One: Golding's novel explores the implications of man's hunger to be accepted by – and to conform to – the group, but also the group's tendency to single-out a scapegoat.

- In the opening chapter, as the boys cast votes for leader, Piggy initially withholds his vote, then 'grudgingly' succumbs and votes in line with the majority: an early instance of the group bending an individual to its will. Yet in many ways Ralph is the most interesting case study when assessing the influence of the group over an individual. While Ralph, the novel's protagonist, is the group's elected leader – and thus in a uniquely powerful position to mould the group as opposed to vice versa – time and again he proves susceptible to the group's whims, and hungry for its affirmation. For instance, he reveals Piggy's nickname, even though Piggy 'said not to tell', to gain social capital; he is swept up in the mock hunt of Robert in Chapter Seven and, perhaps most crucially, he is swept up also in the murder of Simon. Indeed, the sequence that sees the murder of Simon is particularly telling, for it seems to characterise the group as an entity in its own right: the narrator talks of 'the throb and stamp of a single organism', the word 'organism' suggesting the group has a life of its own. [*AO1 for advancing the argument with a judiciously selected quote; AO2 for the close analysis of the language.*]
- The individual's lack of agency in the face of the group, but also the loss of identity that ensues, is communicated through an array of linguistic tactics. Frequently in the novel, for example, speech is left

unattributed – both obscuring the individual behind the speech, and implying that the speech emanates from the group as a whole. [*AO2 for discussing how form shapes meaning.*]

- Yet Golding's novel is not only a meditation on the group's power to sway the individual, but also on the group's hunger to persecute a scapegoat – be it Piggy; Robert in the mock-hunt; Simon, who is cast as the 'beast' in Chapter Nine; or Ralph himself in the novel's finale. Given how, in the years preceding Golding's novel, the world bore witness to the murderous scapegoating of the Nazi regime, it is perhaps unsurprising that this dynamic was one Golding was keen to dissect. [*AO3 for placing the text in historical context.*]

Theme/Paragraph Two: Golding's novel gives insight into man's tendency to become desensitised as a result of violence, and thus how violence often begets further violence.

- While Golding's novel seems to imply that group dynamics are in no small part responsible for violence, it also delves more generally into how smaller-scale acts of violence can desensitise people and beget more (and more extreme) instances of violence. In the early portion of the novel, there are all kinds of taboos surrounding violence: for Jack, when he fails to slaughter the pig in Chapter One, it is the sense of 'the enormity of the knife cutting into living flesh' – whereas for Roger, who intentionally throws stones just wide of a littlun, it is an internalised sense of the repercussions from 'parents and school and policemen and the law.' [*AO1 for advancing the argument with a judiciously selected quote.*]

- Yet Jack's successful kill in Chapter Four functions as a kind of watershed moment in the normalisation of violence, and it is no coincidence that, shortly after, not only does Jack raise his hands to another boy for the first time (he 'st[i]ck[s] his fist into Piggy's stomach', the slaughter of a pig permitting violence towards its human namesake), but there also unfolds a violent mock-hunt of Robert which leaves him 'squeal[ing] in pain.' It is no coincidence either that, following Jack's second kill in Chapter Eight, there is yet another escalation in violence: not only are there instances of deliberate torture, but there are also two murders (of Simon and Piggy) and the attempted murder of Ralph. It seems Golding is suggesting that, while *homo-sapiens* often treat violence as taboo and fear repercussions, once these taboos are violated and fear of retribution removed, there is little in human nature to stop people from engaging in ever more extreme violence. [*AO1 for advancing the argument with a judiciously selected quote; AO2 for the close analysis of the language.*]

Theme/Paragraph Three: Golding's novel is a meditation on the profound sway fiction has over the human psyche.

- At one point in Chapter Seven, while accompanying a small exploratory party to investigate the figure on the mountaintop, Ralph becomes lost in thoughts about the 'the books' on 'the shelf by the bed' in one of his former homes, and the reader learns of the profound impact the stories had on him: we hear how one text, for example, inspired a kind of 'tied-down terror', as the narrator alliteratively puts it. Certainly, this sequence is instructive when assessing an earlier sequence, from Chapter One, in which Ralph proclaims that their situation is 'just like in a book', eliciting a list of famous narratives of stranded children: 'Treasure Island'; 'Swallows and Amazons'. Together, these sequences inform us that the boys perceive the island through an incredibly power fictional prism, and alerts us to their tendency to model their behaviour on fictional paradigms. A case in point is Jack's appropriation of the role of hunter – a part straight out of boyish comics, and which he often enacts fictionally (as well as in reality) in the form of "mock" hunts. Indeed, just prior to Ralph's reflections on his books back home, the narrator observes how Jack 'trod with theatrical caution' while navigating – the word 'theatrical' indicating how Jack-the-Hunter is a role informed by make-believe. [*AO1 for advancing the argument with a judiciously selected quote; AO2 for the close analysis of the language.*]

- If Golding's novel points to the influence fictional texts have over the psyche, it also explores – through the notion that a 'beast' stalks the island – how powerful a word-of-mouth collective fiction can be. Indeed, the fiction of the beast is so powerful that even sceptics, such as Piggy, prove credulous at times of extreme stress ('It's come!...It's real!' he exclaims when he hears Jack sneaking outside his shelter in Chapter Ten). [*AO1 for advancing the argument with a judiciously selected quote; AO2 for the close analysis of the language.*]

- It is important to note that the sway of fictions over the human psyche was a powerful theme in the twentieth century. For example, Jorge Luis Borges's 1940 short story, 'Tlon, Uqbar, Orbis Tertius', is about a fictional world, 'Tlon', that takes such a hold on man's imagination that it seems, over time, to in fact usurp reality. [*AO3 for invoking relevant literary context.*]

Conclusion

"At one point in the novel, Henry – one of the littleuns – intervenes in the lives of the small creatures on the beach with his stick, 'urging them, ordering them' and 'exercising control over living things'. Golding, too, might be argued to be engaging in this same human urge to exert control over the lives of others through the very act of writing the novel: he is tapping into man's yearning for 'the illusion of mastery.' However, while Golding's act of writing might point to the human urge to exert control, it points also to a facet of human nature we have discussed already: namely, our broader tendency to deploy fiction to try and make sense of our lived existence."

ESSAY PLAN SEVEN

HOW DOES JACK EXPLOIT FEAR OF THE BEAST IN LORD OF THE FLIES?

INTRODUCTION

"In many respects, the Weimar Republic succumbed to Nazism in the 1930s as a result of fear: fear of economic hardship in the wake of the Great Depression; fear of communism; fear of ethnic outsiders – the list goes on. Given that Golding intended Jack and his secessionists to be a kind of reincarnation of the Nazi movement, it is unsurprising that a key mechanism Jack uses to take and reconcile power is fear – particularly fear of the beast the children believe to stalk the island. Yet while the beast in some senses seems ubiquitous – fires, snakes, boars, the pilot, and the island itself are all identified as the beast at one point or another – that it is purely fictional seems to be a comment on the fundamental hollowness of the fascist movement."

Theme/Paragraph One: Jack attempts to exploit Ralph's fear of the beast in a bid to subvert him and destabilise his leadership.[1]

- As a group of boys in Chapter Seven travel to the mountaintop at dusk to try and verify Sam and Eric's sighting – they had spotted the pilot's cadaver and mistook it for a monster – Jack exploits Ralph's fear that a beast lies in wait to try and subvert Ralph's standing. That Jack is keen to wrest power is made clear as the sequence unfolds, with Ralph gauging Jack's 'rising antagonism' when Jack is placed to the rear of the search party and thus 'ceased to lead.' In a deft exploitation the boys' tendency to equate leadership with risk-tasking and daring do, Jack then insists that he will persist to the mountaintop – 'I'm going up the mountain' – and challenges Ralph to do the same: 'Coming?' That the challenge is antagonistic is telegraphed through Jack's body-language (the reader is told he held his spear 'as if he threatened Ralph') as well as the other boys' sense that the challenge is 'too successfully daunting' to not take seriously. [*AO1 for advancing the argument with a judiciously selected quote; AO2 for the close analysis of the language.*]
- If this incident represents Jack exploiting Ralph's fear of the beast to try and subvert his status, it ought to be noted that it falls short in various ways: not only does Ralph accept Jack's challenge in a way that meant Jack's taunt 'fell powerless' – the word 'powerless' emphasising how Jack's gambit had been a power-play in the first place – but Ralph is also the one who

approaches the pilot. However, the mere fact Jack successfully forces Ralph to play by his rules – forces Ralph to elevate imprudent risk-taking in order to save face – indicates that Jack's *does* succeed at least up to a point in exploiting Ralph's fear to destabilise his leadership. [*AO1 for advancing the argument with a judiciously selected quote; AO2 for the close analysis of the language.*]

Theme/Paragraph Two: By framing his hunters as a defensive mechanism that will protect the other boys from the beast, Jack is able to exploit rising fear of the beast.

- At one point in Chapter Five, as frenzied conversation about the possibility of a beast derails a meeting, Jack defiantly posits the violence he has at his disposal as an antidote to the beast: 'We're strong – we hunt! If there's a beast, we'll hunt it down!' Not only does the staccato lilt, the exclamation marks, and the hard pause generated by the dash create an almost chant-like air to this assertion, but the repetition of 'we' almost sounds as though a political pitch: the potential 'we' under Jack's leadership – as opposed to Ralph's – has as an answer to the beast.[2] [*AO1 for advancing the argument with a judiciously selected quote; AO2 for the close analysis of the language.*]
- After the airman has been misinterpreted as a beast, however, Jack's exploitation of the rising fear becomes more sophisticated still. While Jack continues to frame the physical prowess of the hunters as a weapon to level against the beast, he also starts to imply,

paradoxically, that it could also be used instead to appease the beast, suggesting that they leave portions of the pigs they hunt – 'some of the kill' – to ensure the beast 'won't bother [them].' Jack has the tools, then, to both battle, but also *bargain with*, the beast. Yet perhaps more sophisticated still is Jack's manoeuvre to exploit the shame the boys feel *as a result* of their fear of the beast, with his provocative and erroneous claim that 'Ralph thinks you're cowards, running away from the boar and the beast.' The subtext is clear: Jack will insulate them not only from the beast, but also their shame. [*AO1 for advancing the argument with a judiciously selected quote; AO2 for the close analysis of the language.*]

- If by Chapter 9 Jack's pitch is explicit – 'My hunters will protect you from the beast. Who will join my tribe?' – it is also moot, since it has already proved successful: Jack has successfully seceded and has all but wrested power from Ralph. [*AO1 for advancing the argument with a judiciously selected quote.*]

Theme/Paragraph Three: Fear of the beast also allows Jack to reconcile power, for he uses it as a mechanism to victimise Simon and, in so doing, normalises the violence that allows him to maintain power.

- During the murder of Simon – one of the novel's most climactic scenes – it is striking that the boys perpetrating the murder, swept up in a frenzy of bloodlust and fear, cast Simon as the elusive beast: the reader hears how 'the beast stumbled into the horseshoe' the boys had created with the bodies; how the 'beast was on its knees'; and how, finally, 'the beast lay still'. Although the narrator seeks to hint at the boys' lack of individual agency with the assertion that they moved as a 'single organism,' Jack – more than any of the others boys – might be said actively exploiting the fear of the others, since he is the one who initiates the dance: 'Do our dance! Come on! Dance!' he proclaims – the repetition of dance not only a literal invitation, but also a nod to the fact the children are now dancing to his metaphorical tune. [*AO1 for advancing the argument with a judiciously selected quote; AO2 for the close analysis of the language.*]

- While all the boys understand on some level that this is Simon, those who then go on to align with Jack prefer to delude themselves with Jack's narrative – '[the beast] came – disguised', Stanley asserts in Chapter Ten – since Jack is offering them the cathartic 'illusion of mastery'. However, if Jack's scapegoating of Simon offers the other boys the illusion of power, it also normalises a violent code of conduct that further allows Jack to reconcile power. Ironically, Jack exploits the boys' fear to create a society predicated on fear, violence and 'irresponsible leadership.' [*AO1 for advancing the argument with a judiciously selected quote; AO2 for the close analysis of the language.*]

Theme/Paragraph Four: While deft at exploiting the other boys' fear, Jack also proves fearful of the

beast – and this arguably causes him to act against his own best interests.

- At one point in Chapter Five, Jack, while deriding the littluns as 'cry-babies and sissies' for fearing the beast, reveals that he too is not impervious to said fear: 'of course we're frightened sometimes but we put up with being frightened.' Indeed, Jack's fear of the beast is on show again when Jack, Ralph and Simon find the cadaver, and Jack is left 'shivering and croaking.' With this in mind, it is arguable that Jack increasingly leans into his role of hunter as a coping mechanism: as a way to 'put up with being frightened'. Yet in many respects his obsession with hunting in fact subverts Jack's own best interests, for in Chapter Four his obsession with the hunt at the expense of maintaining the fire means they squander an opportunity to escape the island. In this reading, then, Jack is less puppet-master exploiting the fear of others, and more the victim of his own fears. [*AO1 for advancing the argument with a judiciously selected quote; AO2 for the close analysis of the language.*]

Conclusion

"For all the boys' efforts to pinpoint the beast, it is Simon – the novel's muted Cassandra – who understands that the beast is ultimately a metaphor for man's capacity for evil: 'However Simon thought of the beast, there rose before his inward sight the picture of a human.'[3] As a result, Jack is not merely the one who most exploits fear of the beast, but who most *embodies* the beast: 'You're a beast and a swine', as Piggy puts it in his final showdown with Jack. Certainly, one can see the influence of Freud in this idea of man's inner beast – more specifically, Freud's writings in the 1920s about the 'id', the realm of the mind that contains our basest, most primal instincts."

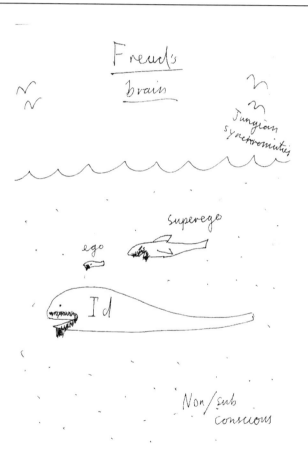

Cartoonist Cachecope Bell's take on the human brain as conceived by Sigmund Freud. Copyright © Cachecope Bell

ESSAY PLAN EIGHT

WHAT ROLE DO THE LITTLUNS PLAY IN LORD OF THE FLIES?

INTRODUCTION

"As Sigmund Freud in the early twentieth century grappled with the psychology of children and infants, there came an inflection point in how society thought of youngsters: their minds were increasingly deemed worthy of discrete study. Golding's novel is deeply interested in the nuances of the child psyche; so much so that its island is populated not just with pre-adolescents, but younger children, too. Yet while these 'littluns' are perhaps most significant as a powerful conduit to the realm of fantasy, they also serve other functions: they place a burden of responsibility on the older children, and act in ways that have profound symbolic resonances."

Theme/Paragraph One: The littluns function to put the biguns in a position of adult responsibility, thereby raising the stakes of the drama.

- If the lack of adult supervision established in the novel's opening chapters ('there aren't any grownups', Ralph proclaims at an early conch meeting) puts the onus on the pre-adolescent children to govern themselves, the presence of the littluns complicates the dynamic, for they implicitly impose on the older children a duty of care. The observation that the littluns responded to Ralph and his conch because 'he was big enough to be a link with the adult world of authority' shines further light on this dynamic: the littluns cast the older children as surrogate adults, and, in so doing, place the 'biguns' (as they come to be known) in a position of 'authority' and responsibility – and much of the novel's drama stems from how they respond to that responsibility. [*AO1 for advancing the argument with a judiciously selected quote; AO2 for the close analysis of the language.*]

- Jack, on the one hand, generally takes a *laissez-faire*, neglectful approach to the littluns – as exemplified by the way his early rush to start a fire almost certainly leads to the death of the boy with the 'mulberry-coloured birthmark' – though he is at times openly antagonistic: he jokes at one point of 'us[ing] a littlun' in a hunt. Yet while Ralph laughs at this joke and occasionally proves neglectful, he largely functions as a counterpoint to Jack, living by the credo that 'someone's got to look after them.' [*AO1 for advancing the argument with a judiciously selected quote.*]

- Yet though the littluns function to highlight how Jack

and Ralph differ in their role of surrogate adult, they also serve to remind us of the older children's youth. At one point, Roger throws stones in the 'space round Henry' – one of the littluns – but avoids hitting him due to internalized deference towards 'parents and school and policemen and the law.' Even as the littluns place the older children in a position of authority, they remind us of the biguns' own need for authority and regulation: the literal 'space round Henry' a metaphor for the void now missing in the older boys' lives. [*AO1 for advancing the argument with a judiciously selected quote; AO2 for the close analysis of the language.*]

Theme/Paragraph Two: The littluns invigorate the realm of fantasy and the imagination, and, in so doing, fuel a belief in the beast in the minds of the older boys.

- At one point, the narrator meditates on one of the littluns – Henry – and how, if he had been told that the boy with the mulberry-coloured birthmark 'had gone home in an aircraft, he would have accepted it without fuss or disbelief.' That Henry is 'without... disbelief' is crucial: the littluns are credulous, and are willing to buy into the realm of fantasy. Indeed, while this instance of credulity may be inconsequential, the littluns' willingness to occupy the realm of fantasy – to live 'without... disbelief' – proves profoundly consequential when it comes to the beast. Simon notes that the littluns talk 'as if...the beastie or the snake-thing was real'; and it is their willingness to believe in the material existence of this fictional entity that seems to breathe life into the myth, and keeps the possibility alive in the minds of the older children. In fact, Jack berates them for just that, asserting that 'you littluns started all this, with the fear talk. Beasts!' While the single-word sentence – 'Beasts!' – is most obviously a reference to the fictional creature the littluns have brought to life, it could also arguably be construed an insult lobbed at the littluns: Jack is resentfully labelling them 'beasts' due to the unsettling and infantilizing effect their fiction-telling has had on him – an effect Jack resents. [*AO1 for advancing the argument with a judiciously selected quote; AO2 for the close analysis of the language.*]

Theme/Paragraph Three: The littluns engage in actions that are steeped in symbolism, and thus offer new ways of decoding the novel.

- While Roger's act of throwing stones at Henry in the aforementioned sequence is profoundly telling, so too is Henry's own activities during this sequence. Henry, using 'a bit of stick', attempts to 'control the motions of' the small sea creatures on the beach: for instance, 'he made little runnels' and 'crowd[ed] them with creatures;' and 'he talked to them, urging them, ordering them' – the accumulation of verbs ('talked', 'urging', 'ordering') emphasising Henry's heightened sense of agency. Henry's dictatorial tactics here, however, are not incidental, but are a symbolic prefiguring of Jack's later attempts to assert a dictatorial rule over the island: in the same way Henry finds escape and happiness in 'exercising control over living things,' so too does Jack, with his later exertions of power. Yet, crucially, the narrator observes that Henry has only 'the illusion of mastery'; likewise, Jack's mastery is always limited by the circumstances – whether adults might arrive (which they eventually do), the physical realities on the island, and so forth – and thus in many senses remains always an 'illusion.' [*AO1 for advancing the argument with a judiciously selected quote; AO2 for the close analysis of the language.*]

- However, if Henry here offers a symbolic foreshadowing of Jack's later attempt to rule by fiat, he also reflects Golding's role as author: the way Golding has 'crowded' the island 'with creatures' in order to give his novel narrative impetus, and to thus satisfy his own yearning for the 'illusion of mastery'.[1] [*AO1 for advancing the argument with a judiciously selected quote; AO2 for the close analysis of the language;.*]

Theme/Paragraph Four: The way the littluns express themselves in a way that bypasses language heightens both the tension and the tragic impact of the novel.

- In Shakespeare's *King Lear* – a play which influenced Golding greatly – the eponymous protagonist, when presented with the body of his daughter Cordelia, is so overcome by the tragedy that language is insufficient to capture his grief, and his only recourse is to howl: 'Howl, howl, howl, howl!'[2] When Percival, one of the littluns, is put forward to talk at a fraught conch discussion about the beast, his ability to articulate himself similarly lapses altogether, and a 'lamentation rose out of him, loud and sustained.' If the word 'lamentation' – a word associated with grief and death – is loaded, perhaps even more so is the assertion that the crying 'seemed to sustain him upright as if he were nailed to it.' In this formulation, Percy becomes an almost Christ-like figure, 'nailed' to his own 'lamentation' as Jesus was the cross – the allusion suggesting that he is living through a tragedy of Christ-like proportions. [*AO1 for advancing the argument with a judiciously selected quote; AO2 for the close analysis of the language; AO3 for placing the text in literary context.*]

- Interestingly, when Jack steals the fire from Ralph's camp – another tragedy, since it compromises their ability to alert help – a littlun again serves a similar function, as the reader is told how 'a littlun howled, creased and crimson.' Yet while the littluns' yells alert us to the tragedy afoot, they function also simply to up the tension: for instance, when Percy, after falling asleep, wakes and screams again – a 'remote and unearthly' scream that, for emphasis, appears at the very close of Chapter Five – the impact as much as anything is to heighten the tension and drama. [*AO1 for advancing the argument with a judiciously selected quote; AO2 for the close analysis of the language.*]

Conclusion

"Piggy, the reader is informed at one point, arrived 'whimpering like a littlun' and in the final pages of the novel we learn how Ralph 'whimpered and yawned like a littlun.' There is great irony in this simile, for although these two biguns are being likened to a distinct separate group – the younger children – the simile up to a point simply short-circuits, for by many measures the biguns *are* still littluns: mere pre-adolescent children. Ultimately this is perhaps the littluns most important function: to remind us that, in the grand scheme, *all* the children are still pre-adolescent littluns – a fact that is arguably the novel's greatest source of drama."

A 1969 Polish film poster for *Lord of the Flies* — from the artist Ryszard Kiwerski.

NOTES

ESSAY PLAN ONE

1. If Ralph's moral code is fungible, it means that it is liable to change.
   Someone's ability to exert agency refers to their ability to exert free will in any given situation.
2. If you are levelling opprobrium at someone it means you are being harshly critical of them.
3. To transgress is to go beyond or exceed what is permissible.
4. To reprimand someone is to tell them off.
5. Prefigure is another word for foreshadow. It is basically when you hint at something that will take place later in the text.
6. To secede is to breakaway to form a new government.
7. Constitutionalism is the belief in government run by a formal set of rules – that is, a constitution.
   The phrase *de facto* basically refers to the fact that nobody has explicitly said within the novel that Ralph's society are analogous to the allied forces – rather, it is something that seems to be the case by default.
   A Manichean struggle means a struggle between good and evil.
8. A pseudo-society means something akin to an imitation of society.
9. When I talk about the narrator's free indirect style, I am referring to the way in which the narrator recounts events in the third person, and yet sometimes seems to be inside Ralph's head, almost as if the narrator has direct access to Ralph's thoughts. We are not being given unmediated first-person access to Ralph's thoughts, but with the free indirect narrative we are being given the next best thing.
10. The idea that Ralph is in an equivocal position suggests that his role/status is deeply uncertain.

ESSAY PLAN TWO

1. To lionise something is to celebrate it and make it seem noble and grand.
2. An existential threat is something that threatens one's very existence.
3. If something is fallacious it is untrue and/or misleading
4. If something is ubiquitous, it means it is everywhere at once.

ESSAY PLAN THREE

1. Someone's bona-fides are their credentials.
2. The denouement of a story/novel is its final climax.
   To appropriate is to take and use something that belongs to someone else.
3. A taboo is something that society thinks should not be said or done.

ESSAY PLAN FOUR

1. A bulwark is like a defensive wall.
2. A non-sequitur is when one idea does not logically follow on from the other.
   Refrain is when a word or phrase is repeated.
3. An allusion is a reference to another text or piece of work.

ESSAY PLAN FIVE

1. *Raison d'être* is a French term and means 'reason to be'.

ESSAY PLAN SEVEN

1. To subvert someone is to undermine them.
2. Staccato, when used to describe language, implies the words or phrases used are short and jarring.
3. Cassandra is a character from Greek mythology. She is famously able to see the truth, but is ignored by all other people.

ESSAY PLAN EIGHT

1. To rule by fiat means to rule in an arbitrary, dictatorial fashion.
2. The word eponymous basically means that the main character in the play has the same name as the play's title.

ACCOLADE PRESS FOR GCSE ENGLISH: THE RANGE

www.accoladetuition.com/accolade-gcse-guides

ENGLISH LITERATURE

Romeo and Juliet: Essay Writing Guide for GCSE (9-1)

Macbeth: Essay Writing Guide for GCSE (9-1)

Power and Conflict: Essay Writing Guide for GCSE (9-1)

Dr Jekyll and Mr Hyde: Essay Writing Guide for GCSE (9-1)

A Christmas Carol: Essay Writing Guide for GCSE (9-1)

The Merchant of Venice: Essay Writing Guide for GCSE (9-1)

Love and Relationships: Essay Writing Guide for GCSE (9-1)

Great Expectations: Essay Writing Guide for GCSE (9-1)

An Inspector Calls: Essay Writing Guide for GCSE (9-1)

Pride and Prejudice: Essay Writing Guide for GCSE (9-1)

The Tempest: Essay Writing Guide for GCSE (9-1)

Unseen Poetry: Essay Writing Guide for GCSE (9-1)

Much Ado About Nothing: Essay Writing Guide for GCSE (9-1)

ENGLISH LANGUAGE

English Language Paper One: A Technique Guide for GCSE (9-1)

English Language Paper Two : A Technique Guide for GCSE (9-1)

If you found this book useful, please consider leaving a review on Amazon, which you can do at the following link: **https://rcl.ink/FVDsh**

You can also join our private Facebook group (where our authors share resources and guidance) by visiting the following link: **https://rcl.ink/DME.**

Printed in Great Britain
by Amazon